AWESOME HERBS FOR KIDS

Botany
Herbs and spices

All rights reserved. No part of this publication may be reproduced, distributed, or transmitted in any form or by any means All rights reserved. No part of this publication may be reproduced, distributed, or transmitted in any form or by any means. ©

All Rights Reserved.

Basil

If you drink me, I will improve your mood, and protect you from depression.

Anise

I can help you treat stomach gas, and breath shortness problems.

Arugula

I have vitamins and minerals that help treat hair loss.

Mint

I'm a sedative, and if you inhale me every day I will promote respiratory health.

Flax

If you want to lose weight use me, I can also treat your diarrhea.

Sage

I fight free radicals that cause inflammation and cancer.

Parsley

A hot cup of me helps you fight kidney stones.

Mustard seed

My job is to relieve joint pain and rheumatism.

Liquorice

Trust me, I will treat you if you have a sore throat and cough.

Fennel

If you want to keep your bones healthy and strong you should eat me.

Dill

I have antimicrobial and antibacterial properties.

Garlic

You should know that I am the most powerful anti-cancer in the world so far.

Oregano

I will help you destroy skin infections.

Thyme

I greatly contribute to raising the immunity of the respiratory system.

Celery

Scientists have confirmed that my juice helps treat infections, muscle cramps, colds and influenza.

Chicory

I have effective diabetes prevention properties if you take me as a drink.

Leek

Many people consider me the best hair loss solution if you want to have a strong hair use me.

Nettles

You can use my vital properties to treat anemia also all anxiety disorders.

Chamomile

I am the best natural sedative, if you want to sleep comfortably, take a cup of me every night.

Chives

Anyone who eats me raw, will cleanse his gut of harmful microbes.

Lettuce

Everyone loves me because I don't cause any side effects, I will keep your stomach healthy just trust me.

Ginger

Many people use me to strengthen the immune system and prevent heart disease.

Turmeric

I'm more like ginger, but darker in my color, i'm a anti-inflammatory and immune-booster.

Coriander

I'm one of the most effective herbs in lowering bad cholesterol levels.

Cumin

I will help you maintain a healthy liver by improving the secretion of digestive enzymes.

Saffron

Recent scientific studies have proven my benefits in treating Alzheimer's and forgetfulness problems.

Dandelion

If you suffer from chronic or recurring constipation, you should use me.

Aloe

I can treat your dry skin problems.

Don't forget to use us after consulting an herbal expert.

BYE!

Printed in Great Britain
by Amazon